ECONOMY IN ACTION!

MONEY MATTERS

83356 A

UNITED STATES · WHICH
FEDERAL RESERVE SYS

THIS NOTE IS LEGAL TEN
FOR ALL DEBTS, PUBLIC AND

Treasurer of the

10

Treasurer of the United States.

BreAnn Rumsch

ABDO Publishing Company

visit us at
www.abdopublishing.com

Published by ABDO Publishing Company, PO Box 398166, Minneapolis, MN 55439. Copyright © 2013 by Abdo Consulting Group, Inc. International copyrights reserved in all countries. No part of this book may be reproduced in any form without written permission from the publisher. The Checkerboard Library™ is a trademark and logo of ABDO Publishing Company.

Printed in the United States of America, North Mankato, Minnesota.
052012
092012

Cover Photo: Corbis
Interior Photos: AP Images pp. 11, 13, 20; Corbis pp. 9, 15, 25; Getty Images pp. 5, 6, 8; iStockphoto pp. 18, 23, 28; Thinkstock pp. 1, 7, 17; United States coin images from the United States Mint p. 10; US National Archives and Records Administration p. 27

Editors: Tamara L. Britton, Megan M. Gunderson
Art Direction: Neil Klinepier

Library of Congress Cataloging-in-Publication Data

Rumsch, BreAnn, 1981-
 Money matters / BreAnn Rumsch.
   p. cm. -- (Economy in action!)
 Includes index.
 ISBN 978-1-61783-489-9
 1. Money--Juvenile literature. I. Title.
 HG221.5.R86 2013
 332.4--dc23
                          2012014365

Contents

World of Money

Every day, money is exchanged across the globe. It pays for gifts, new clothes, school supplies, and each meal you eat. It makes businesses run and communities thrive. In short, money makes the world go around!

Do you have five dollars somewhere? What is that money worth to you? Perhaps it's worth a pack of trading cards or a new tube of lip gloss. Maybe it's worth a comic book or a cute headband. The truth is, money is only worth what we are willing to exchange for it.

The value of money, goods, and services changes over time. This change is influenced by the economy. That may sound like grown-up stuff. But it applies to you, too!

You take part in the economy every time you choose how to use your money. So keep reading to better understand the world of money and why it matters.

What is your money worth to you?

What Is Money?

So what exactly is money, anyway? Simply put, money is anything people accept as a trade for goods or services. When money is used in this way, it is known as a medium of exchange.

Beads made from shells and stone were once used as money. They were also prized for their decorative value.

The modern money you use includes metal coins and paper bills. It is known as currency.

Every country has a basic unit of currency. In the United States, it is the US dollar. In Mexico, it is the peso. Canada uses the Canadian dollar. And, many European countries use the euro.

Early humans had no use for currency. They met their needs by hunting, gathering, and **bartering**. Later, people used beads, shells, and stones as money. These items are very different from quarters, nickels, and dimes! But, they have something in common. The people exchanging them consider them valuable.

As civilizations became more advanced, forms of payment changed. Foods, weapons, animals, and metals were **bartered**. These products were known as commodity money. This is because they weren't just useful as money. They were also useful as goods.

Eventually, people wanted to trade more easily. To allow for constant buying and selling, a new money system was developed. We still use it today!

MONEY PROFILE

Objects used as money share several qualities.

1. They must be strong and easy to move around.

2. People must be able to count them.

3. They must be familiar, yet rare in supply.

Grains traded as money held extra value as food.

Gold to Green

The first metal coins were made during the 600s BC in modern-day Turkey. They were made of electrum. Over time, gold, silver, and other metals were also used to make coins.

The Chinese invented paper money as early as the AD 600s. In the United States, paper money was first used by Massachusetts colonists in 1690. It was cheaper to make than coins. So, it grew in popularity.

In 1792, the Coinage Act gave the US dollar a set value against gold and silver. This meant that one dollar in currency could be traded for one dollar's worth of gold or silver.

Electrum coins

FUN FACT

In the early 1800s, there were many gold rushes! As a result, gold supplies grew more plentiful around the world.

New money couldn't be created without new gold and silver to give it value. So, this metal standard helped to steady the dollar's worth.

Then in 1900, the Gold Standard Act set a fixed **exchange rate** between countries using the gold standard. A silver standard was also sometimes used.

In 1937, US gold holdings were moved for safekeeping. Today, the Bullion Depository at Fort Knox, Kentucky, holds nearly 150 million ounces (4 million kg) of gold.

Today, coins and paper money can no longer be exchanged for gold or silver. Why? A fiat system of money was eventually considered best. But fiat money has no value! It is simply guaranteed by the government as legal to use.

The fiat system means paper money no longer needs to be backed by precious metal. So, there is no limit to how much money can be created and exchanged. The fiat system lets the money supply grow as the economy grows!

You now know that the money supply grows with the economy. Yet, coins and bills represent just a small amount of the world's money. Numbers in bank accounts around the world represent much more.

Still, creating physical money remains important. So who's in charge of that? In the United States, this task belongs to the US Department of the Treasury.

The Treasury was started in 1789. In 1792, it set up the first US mint to create coin money. Since then, eight mints have operated at different times. Today, only two create coins for general use. Most coins are made in Philadelphia, Pennsylvania. The rest are made in Denver, Colorado.

Take a look at the coins around your home. You will see either a P or a D marked on each of them. This letter tells you which mint created that coin.

The US Treasury began printing paper money in 1861. The following year, it set up the Bureau of Engraving and Printing (BEP). In 1877, the BEP became responsible for all printed money.

Printing money is a detailed process. The BEP's special method makes US bills look and feel **unique**. Numerous security features are included. They protect the money from being **counterfeit**.

US bills are printed on paper made of cotton and linen.

Money Supply

The US Treasury works closely with the Federal Reserve System, or the Fed. As the nation's central bank, the Fed manages the country's money supply. When this is done well, the economy is healthy. Prices stay steady, businesses grow, and workers stay employed.

Sometimes though, the Fed cannot prevent a financial crisis. In 2007, the United States experienced the start of its worst **recession** in 70 years.

After a crisis, the money supply is no longer in balance. So, recovery can take a long time. Banks have less money to loan. And, many workers experience **unemployment**. Businesses also suffer because people stop spending money.

These imbalances can create a snowball effect, each making the other worse. At such times, the government may try to help.

FUN FACT

The Fed was started in 1913.

12

The American Recovery and Reinvestment Act helped pay for projects such as roadwork. These projects improved communities and provided jobs.

Usually, it raises or lowers **interest** rates. It can also use federal money to help **stimulate** economic activity.

For example, President Barack Obama signed the American Recovery and Reinvestment Act in 2009. It aimed to create new jobs and reduce some debts.

Around the same time, the Fed approved giving money to banks. This helped banks continue loaning to consumers. With these loans, people were able to buy cars or homes. Their purchases supported many businesses across the nation.

Big Spender

After money is created, it is earned, spent, and saved. Members of a society hold jobs to help an economy produce goods and services. In return, they earn money. This is purchasing power!

To buy goods and services, we know to check their prices. Businesses use prices to tell you how much you will need to spend for something. Spending can be fun! But, remember to take care of your needs before your wants.

Huh? What are needs and wants? Needs are things you must have to survive, such as shelter and food. Wants are everything else! Everybody's list of wants is different. Yours may include a new video game or a cell phone.

As a spender, you will learn that all choices have costs. Choosing to spend money on one thing means giving up the chance to spend it on something else. This is called opportunity

FUN FACT

Needs and wants are also called necessities and luxuries.

cost. The best way to understand this concept is to understand wants versus needs.

We often must choose our needs over our wants. This is called resource allocation. When you spend money, businesses thrive! But you still have a responsibility to spend wisely.

Everyone has a **finite** amount of resources to live off of. So learn to spend as well as save and invest. This will put you on the road to a bright financial future.

Wants can be tricky because they often seem like needs. For instance, you need shoes. But the style you choose is a want.

Credit Careful

Do you remember why the modern money system was developed? It allows for constant buying and selling! Well, credit takes this idea one step further.

Credit allows people to spend money when they may not actually have it. Like money, credit holds value. It is given based on **confidence** that a borrower can pay the loan back.

Used correctly, credit is a powerful tool. For example, commercial credit helps new businesses get started. And consumer credit helps people buy homes or cars. Banks often lend money to borrowers for these purchases.

The bank is known as the creditor. The borrower is known as the debtor. He or she pays back the loan on a schedule over time. The bank also gets something in return for putting its money at risk. So, borrower payments include **interest**.

You may also be familiar with credit cards. Using them can be a great way to buy things. But, this is only true as long as interest charges are avoided.

If your mom buys something with a credit card, the credit card company pays the store. Then, it sends her a bill. By paying the bill in full each month, she will avoid **interest**. This is a good way to manage monthly spending.

Unfortunately, it is very easy to overspend with credit cards. People who owe more than they can pay may make a minimum payment. The remaining balance is carried over to the next month's bill. This is known as revolving debt.

The longer it takes to pay off the bill, the more interest is paid. These extra fees mean less money is available for spending on needs and wants.

For US credit cards, the average interest rate is 14.45%. At this rate, a $1,000 balance could take six years to pay off with minimum monthly payments. The total owed would equal $1,540!

Fiscally Fit

Fiscal fitness has nothing to do with lifting weights and running the mile! Instead, this type of fitness exercises your knowledge about money.

One of the most important lessons to learn is how to live within your means. You already know how to spend money. But what about making sure you don't spend too much?

Many families create a budget. This is a plan for how money is earned and spent over a period of

Good habits can help you avoid debt. By saving first, you can pay cash for your purchases.

time. A budget can also help you make choices between needs and wants.

Remind yourself of your list of needs versus wants. Then check the budget. Do you have enough money for your needs? How much money is left? This amount can be spent on your wants.

Sometimes, it makes more sense to save that extra money than to spend it. Perhaps you've had your eye on the latest iPod. One week's allowance isn't going to pay for an expensive item like that! So, you will have to save for a while.

Saving can be a challenge at first because it requires delayed gratification. Waiting for what we want is not easy.

But learning to save is one of the most important things you'll ever do. Why? It allows you to increase your buying power! After a few months, you'll have enough money set aside to buy the iPod. What a great reward for the patience you practiced!

GROWING MORE MONEY

Did you know that a job isn't the only way to earn money? That's right! The money you have can actually earn you more money. Thanks to interest, money you save in the bank can grow. Investing is another way to grow your money. It has a higher risk than saving, but it can yield greater rewards.

Scarcity

You know money allows people to exchange goods and services. So whether it's cash or credit, money drives the economy. Money sounds like a great thing! So why don't people have all the money they want?

Did you decide to spend your money on concert tickets? What did you give up in order to go?

If money were given freely to everyone, there would be too much! It would compete to buy too few available goods and services. So, prices would increase.

Resources are simply limited. No one, not even the Queen of England, has unlimited resources! There will never be enough time, money, or goods and services to satisfy all our needs and wants. This situation is known as scarcity.

Scarcity is related to **supply** and **demand**. Suppose your favorite band is coming to town for a concert. There are only 500 tickets available, so the supply is 500. If 2,000 people want to go to the concert, the demand is 2,000.

In this situation, demand outweighs supply. The tickets are scarce. Not everyone who wants some will get them. Still, you may find yourself with the option to buy tickets. Lucky you! Just remember that they are not the only resource to consider.

Your money is also a resource. Because of scarcity, we all have to make choices with our money. So, next you have to decide if you are willing to pay for the tickets. Based on your resources, they may prove to be too costly.

Hard Times

Sometimes scarcity requires more serious choices. Some people may not have a choice between wants and needs. They may have to choose between needs.

When money is scarce, resources become limited. During hard times, money that was already set aside can be a huge help. Savings can help people stretch their resources to meet their current needs.

Yet, many people don't think to save until it's too late. During times of **unemployment**, these people may be unable to meet all of their basic needs. Without savings, they may not be able to afford food. Those who cannot pay their **mortgages** may lose their homes.

Do you remember that all choices have costs? During difficult times, opportunity cost goes up. Resources must be used carefully to pay for the most vital needs. Can you imagine giving up ice cream? You might be willing to if it meant being able to buy bread or eggs.

People who cannot support themselves must rely on help from others. Special organizations try to offer aid and support.

Some people are not able to support themselves. Giving to charity can help them make ends meet.

In the United States, government programs also help provide food, housing, and health care. But the more people that are **unemployed**, the bigger the government's burden to help grows.

Even though you can't control economic changes, you can control your resources. By saving money during good times, you will create a safety net. This money will be there to help you through times of scarcity.

Debt

Unemployment is not the only cause of hard times. You already learned why it is important to not overspend. And, you understand that credit must be used carefully. When a person borrows too much, debt leads to limited resources.

So you can see that credit and debt go hand in hand. Part of borrowing is knowing how much credit you can safely use. You should also know how long it will take for you to pay back the debt.

Did you know there is good debt and bad debt? Good debt is usually a loan for college or a **mortgage** for a house. Bad debt often results from using credit cards to pay for wants.

Taking on debt is a big deal! **Defaulting** on payments can have serious consequences, such as **bankruptcy**. Declaring bankruptcy makes it very difficult to get new credit from lenders.

Individuals aren't the only ones dealing with debt. The US government also carries debt. The national deficit is the amount of money the government spends beyond what it earns. The money may fund programs such as welfare and the military.

The national deficit gets paid down by a second type of debt. Selling bonds creates money for the government. But bonds are promises to someday repay bond holders. The amount owed makes up the national debt. In Canada, this is known as the federal government debt.

Some people may think a new car loan is taking on bad debt.
Still, your parents may need that car to get to work!

Tax Time

Financial health can be a difficult goal for people to reach and maintain. Some people face more challenges than others. This is one of the main reasons for taxes. Taxes allow the government to spread around the economy's wealth.

All money spent and earned is taxed in various ways. There are three main types of taxes. They are income tax, property tax, and sales tax.

Income tax is a portion of the money people earn at their jobs. Paying this tax is part of the US **Constitution**! The Sixteenth Amendment became law in 1913.

People who own land and buildings pay property tax. The amount is based on the value of their property.

Does it sound like taxes don't apply to you? Think again! When you spend money, some of it may go to sales tax. Different products are taxed at different rates. The amount depends on the good or service and where you live.

FUN FACT

Many countries outside the United States, including Canada, use a value added tax. Known as a VAT, it is built into the prices paid for goods and services.

With tax money, the government funds certain programs to take care of its people. Poor people may receive aid. Roadways and schools can be built. Police and emergency services can operate.

Paying taxes is just one way you are part of the economy. Every time you earn, spend, or save, you affect the economy.

With time and practice, you will know the best ways to use your resources to meet your needs. You'll probably even figure out how to fulfill a few wants along the way!

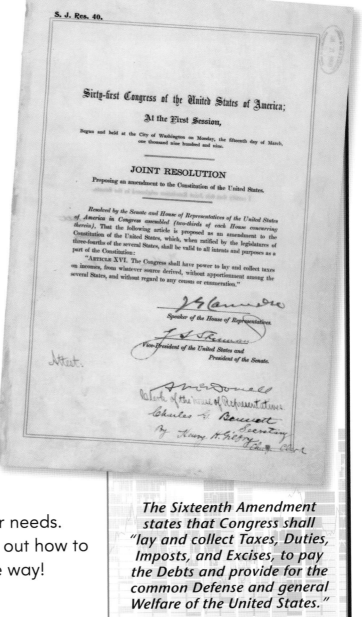

The Sixteenth Amendment states that Congress shall "lay and collect Taxes, Duties, Imposts, and Excises, to pay the Debts and provide for the common Defense and general Welfare of the United States."

THE REAL DEAL

Many security features help keep US printed money safe from fakes. These features vary by denomination. Find some bills and see how many features you can spot.

a) A portrait watermark. When held up to light, this can be seen from the front or back of the bill.

b) Color shifting ink. This ink changes from green to copper on $10, $20, and $50 bills when tilted.

c) Symbols of freedom. Each denomination's symbols are different.

d) Serial Numbers. These appear twice on the front of the bill.

*A vertical security thread is another important feature. Hold your bill up to the light to find it!

MONEY MATCH

Match the currency to the right country!

1. Italy	a) rupee
2. India	b) peso
3. Turkey	c) euro
4. China	d) rand
5. Japan	e) yen
6. Mexico	f) lira
7. South Africa	g) renminbi

Answer Key:
1. c 2. a 3. f 4. g 5. e 6. b 7. d

POWER OF THE US DOLLAR

England	0.63
Italy	0.76
Australia	0.96
China	6.30
Mexico	13.09
India	51.45

Exchange rates change daily. These are from April 17, 2012. Find today's rates online or in your local newspaper.

Not all units of currency are created equal. Some are stronger than others. How much do you think one US dollar (1.00) is worth in currencies from other countries? Take a look to see how it stacks up.

29

Glossary

bankruptcy - the state of having been legally declared unable to pay a debt.

barter - to trade goods or services without using money.

confidence - the state or feeling of being certain.

Constitution - the laws that govern the United States.

counterfeit (KAUNT-uhr-fiht) - an exact copy of something made to trick people.

default - failure to pay money that is owed.

demand - the amount of an available product that buyers are willing and able to purchase.

exchange rate - a number that is used to determine the difference in value between money from different countries.

finite - having limits.

interest - money paid for the use or borrowing of money.

mortgage (MAWR-gihj) - a legal agreement in which a person borrows money to buy property such as land or a house. He or she pays back the money over a period of years.

recession - a period of time when business activity slows.

stimulate - to excite to activity or growth or to greater activity.

supply - the amount of something available for sale.

unemployment - the state of being out of work. Someone who is out of work is unemployed.

unique - being the only one of its kind.

Web Sites

To learn more about the economy in action, visit ABDO Publishing Company online. Web sites about money matters are featured on our Book Links page. These links are routinely monitored and updated to provide the most current information available.

www.abdopublishing.com

Index